Glory & Growth

Kourtney Fullard

BookLeaf Publishing

India | USA | UK

Presentation by *BookLeaf Publishing*

Web: www.bookleafpub.com

E-mail: info@bookleafpub.com

ISBN: 9789363309555

First edition 2024

Holy Necessary (Pruning Season)

Last week, I pruned almost all of my geranium
Though it was big and bushy--
It wasn't healthy
Wasn't thriving
So with my sharp new shears--
I snipped.
Cut off the portions that had blossoms
Though the buds had not -- as of yet -- been
upturned.
Left one stalk still standing
One bright blossom still
stretching toward the sun --
And the side table has since never looked better.

Like it -- I want the Vinedresser to
Rid me of my business -- leaving
only what is bright -- that which is true --

and W(hol)ly necessary.

Womb of Mercy (Racham)

"I will set you in a cleft of the rock, and I will
cover you." Exodus 33:22

Mother me.

Hold me in the round warmth
of your glory.

Speak to me with the firm voice
that sang the universe into living.

Cradle me in the hands that hold
life's skeins taut.

Cover me.

Like the smooth shell of almond,
the canopy of a cool wood,
the quilt of an aged grandmother,
or yellow ochre smoothed over canvas.

Hide me.

In the safe space of the womb
that is your heart.

Discipleship

I never liked following people's example
because my self was already stolen
so why abandon me more
to become like someone else?

But watching these folks,
most likely in their 70s,
(doing what looks like Tai Chi
in the middle of West Philly)
mimicking one another
so much so you can't tell
who is teacher--
reminds me of Ezekiel's wheels*.

Beings moving
in Tandem
in the same Spirit
with the same Essence
for the same glorious purpose.

*Ezekiel 1:19-21

Long Breath

You bear, calmly,
each day I choose worry over
the worthiness of You.

You bear, quietly,
each day I worship the altar
of human approval
over worship at the seat of Mercy.

You wait, with eternal inhale,
for me to relinquish the grip of trauma
and embrace the grasp of Grace.

Regret

Like something undigested--
sending tiny rumblings as
careful reminders of
the steps you missed
in a recipe --
it haunts you.

But instead,
let the reminder
become teacher--
shed light on its' shadow.

Transform it from
leech to lesson.

Life

Warmth;
A burning star calling me. You. A seed. A water
droplet.

From me, a pause on the sidewalk resulting in a
smile.
From you, an extra coating of chocolate brown.
The seed, a tendril twirling up towards light.
The droplet, simple science; evaporation.

Is there not this same warmth in Christ?
Is there not life in His word?

It calls stone to flesh.
Reanimates the paralyzed soul.
Commands gardens to grow from graves.
Transforms a friend from a slave.
Brings abundant freedom to the bound.
Cultivates silence into sound.

Separates life from death;
Gives dead dirt living breath.

Shiloah

There is supernatural power in earth;
the unseen source of Ocean's deep.

How does it keep flowing, moving, surging?
Where does its motion come from?

How is it that living organisms live within it
And swim in places we are not permitted to go?

Where did geysers, glaciers, springs, and
fountains
get their beginning?

From whom did they receive their flow?

Jesus Walked

The one who carved the descent of waterfalls,
Personally planted the sycamore and the cypress,
Who stokes the fires of red giants,
And commands the reins of hurricane wind--
Is the same one who walked the dusty, long
roads of Jerusalem.

The Sublime One--The Only One
With the ability to harness the power of a
Thousand suns
Who could peer through the darkness of a
thousand nights

Walked.
At human speed.

Slowly,
Sweating,
Under the heat of One sweltering sun.

Delighted in a soft breeze
Glided His hand over the fuzz of wheat
Inhaled the very wind He commanded
and became dependent upon it for air.

This same Jesus,
Who spoke the world into being,
Submitted himself to the same natural law
He had dominion over

Treaded gently upon the very ground
He created human life from.

There Is No Color Without Light

In the eye,
there are over 3 million cones (and rods)
responsible for perceiving light
and color.

They are minutely (and microscopically)
situated
so we may receive the gift
of sight

Allowing us to strategically place
our best teal purse
with our choicest white linen dress.

These cones (and rods)
are what makes an outfit "nice"
and pleasing.

Faith, too, is what attracts the eye of God
to man (and vice versa)

Just as color without cones (and rods) is
imperceptible,
so too is the

reality,
understanding,
and sheer pleasure of the Creator
without Faith.

Metamorphosis (A monologue with the Creator)

Forgiveness is weird.
You mean to tell me
That when I mess up
You are "willing" to never bring it up again?
You mean, You not gonna hold this against me?

It is said that babies show
the experiences, attitudes, and behaviors
of their caretakers
(meaning the ones who hold, in their hands, a
baby's needs)
on their faces.

So in reality--I haven't seen You as a caretaker.
I've seen You more as a care...denyer--
Misinterpreting Your gaze of desire as a glare of
disdain.

But yeah...
Compassion is weird.
You mean to tell me
You feel (inwardly) how a pregnant mother feels
for her unborn baby?

It is said that in relationship
honesty,
vulnerability,
trust,
and safety unfurl only in
compassionate, loving and merciful ground.

So in reality--I haven't known you as
a warm sunlight where I can expose my disease
but instead as a harsh fluorescent spotlight
where all my dirt is put on display.

The mind is weird.
You mean to tell me that the way I see You
is shaped by trauma and misconception?

It is said that a man has spent 50 years
Taking his father's face off of yours.

So in reality--I don't really know you.
I only know my experiences.
But in this moment, Your smile is telling me
"Daughter, die to your experiences
so that you can live in the
(Real)ity of Me."

The Real Me.

The Health Benefits of Sucrose

Growth isn't always pleasant.

The truth is
Processed sugar is delicious
And unhealthy feels secure
Because its predictable.

Burning feels like a hearth
when it's all you've ever known.

OdontoGenesis

Beginning something new, as an adult,
Is not unlike losing a baby tooth

I lost my last when I was 12--
Eating pizza and reading "Phillip Hall likes me,
I reckon maybe"
I was happy.
"Barefoot on dirty wooden floor" happy
"Looking in the mirror, mouth gaping
unashamedly" happy
Because this was not just any baby tooth--
It was my last.

I'm beginning again now,
Though that mirth is missing,

I want it back.
I want it with me this time.

For though it feels as if I'm dying--
It's just a new tooth emerging,

Through a tender gum.

Sweet Shame

Shame is saccharine; like the tar baby
Treacly, yet not sweet--though it kills the soul
Sticks to you like honey to a tea cloth

Precious, floral, spun from cotton--that cloth
Is that not too how one should describe soul
small. delicate. precious, like baby

Born to be loved, shame sticks to the dear soul
Telling it lies; tangling like swaddling cloth
Lending pressure, yet discomforts baby

But, Baby threw off cloth and saved soul!

Fluid Seasons

A longing unfulfilled is Autumn
When leaves once verdant and secure, Fall
The creak of branches signaling tears release

Sometimes wisdom calls for release
of leaves and sometimes you find Autumn
where summer should be. Even verdant leaves
fall

at the right time, since seasons choose where
they'll fall.
We can't control the weather. So I lean, release,
when the branch can no longer sustain the
leaf--its Autumn

I learn to release control, so I too may fall, and
become Autumn.

Hosea 14

I've never before seen an ancient Cypress
and up until now I've never truly blossomed.

For much of my life I've been a Lily,
yet half-opened. Subtly scented
not quite fully fragrant.

I've never seen an ancient Cypress.
But, you told Hosea to tell your family
You'd be to them a thriving Cypress. That their
fruit
would come from You.

And you say the same to me
across a span of 4,000 years
You desire to be
Bloom of my Blossom--the very scent of my
fragrance.

A Poem For Humans

I thought I loved you--
our pictures said it all.
I hate how wounds pretend.
Trauma blinds and turns
desire into deception. It was a
good love. Devoid of regular deceit.
Full of wounded dream and
hidden bleeding hearts.
Mine is crusting over--the proteins
are working. If you look beneath
the band-aid-you'll find nothing bitter.
Just dry smiling sadness. That we had to be
lessons. Instead of lovers for life.

Righteous Healing

I thought healing would be
waking up in a linen nightgown
to a beam of morning
towards which I'd stretch my hands,
smile,
then tend to the day in graceful perfection
fully mature and physically immaculate.

But sometimes, healing is making the same
mistakes
over, over, and over again
Asking the maker of Sun
to stretch your hands
toward His graceful perfection.

Sometimes healing is facing your deficits of
immaturity
then turning to the one made mature in suffering
that He may show you which foot to place
on His well-trodded trail blazed path.

A path forged with Spirit's fire;
washed in Holy Blood.

Always, healing is ugly.

On this side of eternity, it has to be
that we may groan tired of this imperfect
raiment
And long to be clothed with Righteousness.

For The Wild Ones Part I

"For My Sisters Who Have Left The Faith"

I know.

Where is the room for my bleeding in this
religion?
In this church?
Am I forced, as I was in my father's house,
to shrink in my Heavenly Father's house?

Where is the room for my yearning?
Must I cover it and hide it (again)
Must I assume the deficits of ones who can't
manage their appetites?
So I must manage it for them, by denying my
own.
Must I fear my sexuality?

And where is the evidence of magic?
Must I connect with an unseen being in
mundane,
systematic ways? Powerless rituals?

Where is the sparkle of joy?
The tingle of healing?

Where is the thrill of freedom?

How is this "religion" different from all I've
experienced?
How can I surrender to a God who feels like
everything else?

How can I practice dead religion when I'm built
for the miraculous?

For The Wild Ones Part II

But in your desire, there is error.
For the walk was never about religion
Or powerless ritual. But life supernatural
Life sempieternal
Wonder that inspires rain to fall, hearts
To race, light to warm, music to swell.

Beauty lives in the invisible and there
Is power in the blood. (Don't you know all we
see was made from what was spoken?)

There is room for the atoms of your soul,
soothing for your anguish, transformation for
your spirit, (and even transcendence).

But we need anchoring, (fairies like us!)
With yearnings to be caught up in God
He's given us limits to glory.

With souls
Wild as ours,
we need tethering to check our wonder.

For The Wild Ones Part III

And though my mind (our minds)
have always had wings (developed that we may
transcend chaos
Though inevitably we were amidst it), we craved
grounding.

So we flocked to law and legality
Convinced it meant tethering
and traded our wings for weights,
mistaking them for stability.

For The Wild Ones Part IV

...but what we really wanted were roots
not religion. But where do we think the wildness
of our spirits come from? we are rivers rushing,
yet even those need banks.
And trees swaying in the wind need grounding.

He gave form, shape, and order to the disarray
and
Lumen to the darkness--made it better.

Gave it purpose.

So too for us, the wild ones..

Your destiny needs a road but you've mistaken it
for a rope.
Just as your glory needs a robe but you've seen it
as a shackle.

(To a wild one, any bearing becomes
burdensome)

But err not in believing you know the direction
For even though wise, the wild can be led astray.

There's beauty in the wild but there's healing in
holiness.
Let Holy hold you then you'll know what
freedom truly means.

Freedom is a warm embrace, more than a wild
release.